NURSED IN THE DESERT
The Prophet Muhammad for Little Hearts

By
SANIYASNAIN KHAN

ILLUSTRATED BY GURMEET

Goodword Books Pvt. Ltd.
1, Nizamuddin West Market
New Delhi-110 013
Tel. 2435 6666, 2435 5454
Fax 9111-2435 7333, 2435 7980
E-mail: info@goodwordbooks.com
Website: www.goodwordbooks.com

Goodwordkidz

Helping you build a family of faith

First published 2003
© Goodword Books 2003

The Prophet Muhammad ﷺ was born in Makkah about 1400 years ago. In those days, it was the custom in Makkah for mothers to send their babies to the desert.

2

There the babies were nursed by paid
foster mothers from among the people
who tended sheep.

5

The weather in the desert, away from the city, was thought to be healthier.

Aminah, the mother of the Prophet Muhammad ﷺ, did this also. So the little Muhammad ﷺ spent the first years of his life with a woman named Halimah and her family of the Banu Sa'd tribe.

Halimah worried that she would not be able
to care properly for the baby Muhammad ﷺ.

They were very poor, and because of the previous year's famine, she had hardly enough milk to feed her own baby.

But as soon as she began nursing Muhammad ﷺ, her milk increased. Things began to change for the better. The land became green, and the date palms grew heavy with fruit. Dates were one of the family's main foods.

The sheep and camels regained their health. Halimah and her husband knew that these blessings were because of the baby Muhammad ﷺ.

Muhammad ﷺ grew well during his stay
with Halimah and her family.

He played with her children, and
together they would take the
sheep to graze.

When Muhammad ﷺ returned to his mother Aminah, he was a strong and healthy three-year-old.

In this way the Prophet Muhammad ﷺ spent the first years of his life in the desert.

ﷺ *Sallal lahu alayhi wa sallam* 'May peace and Allah's blessings be on him.' The customary blessings on the Prophet Muhammad.

Printed in Indi